Leach

浸出

Contents

We have a way

Love

Energy, what is that

Attention

Consciousness

Harboring

L.E.A.C.H.

China ways

So we meet this creature

Going a certain way

Leaking

Beast

We have a way

我们有办法

All we do is teal the energy

我们所要做的就是吸收能量

So after a push of that chi we stay in calm

所以在推开那个气之后，我们保持冷静

Now that we know about that way we must do that in a persi

现在，我们知道了这种方式，我们必须以波斯方式做到这一点。

Let us now do this without going to a Tai Chi mastery

现在让我们无需太极拳就能做到这一点

We stand with feet apart, lucky and smiling a natti

我们分开站着，幸运并微笑着

Oh / 哦

Love

爱

There we have a girl we adore this day

那天我们有一个喜欢的女孩

She looks a bit like a Korean madam

她看起来有点像韩国夫人

We postpone a judgement and feel universal love for her

我们推迟判决并感到对她的普遍爱

She is called Karin, a Dutch girl

她叫'*Karing*', 荷兰女孩

A hart opens and a sunna string energy line connects with her

牡鹿打开, 圣娜弦能量线与她连接

That is love in connection / 那就是联系中的爱

Energy, what is that

能源，那是什么

The chi

气

We move through the chi, the force, if you are a USA persona

如果您是美国角色，我们将穿越气势，力量

The chi can be moved to move other bodies to a warmer or colder banna

可以移动气管以将其他物体移动到较暖或较冷的香蕉上

How to do this is a China way and a USA movie dallu

如何做到这一点是中国方式和美国电影《大路》

The secret is that we all have that energy around and in, we are it

秘诀是我们周围和内部都有能量，就是这样

There is some pain if you push too hard / 不要太用力推气

Attention

注意

Look at the woman at the cover of this international book, Karin

看看这本国际书籍封面上的女人,卡琳

Give some look to her eyes and her nose and her eyes ag.

看一下她的眼睛,鼻子和眼睛。

Now, feel like you are looking through her beauty eyes, you can

现在,感觉就像您透过她美丽的眼睛看时,

There is attention from you, you connect your chi to her picture look

有你的注意,你把你的气与她的照片相联系

Now you are also connected with an assu chi line to her

现在,您还与她的阿苏池线相连

She can now feel that / 她现在可以感觉到

Consciousness

意识

Are you so high conscious that you feel all in your body

您的意识如此强烈,以至于感觉到自己的全部

If you are lower conscious you only feel your fingers move

如果您意识不清,只会感觉到手指在动

Now breath through your nostrils and be calm for an hour

现在,呼吸一下鼻孔,保持冷静一个小时

What happens to the feeling of how you meet the chi in you

您如何认识自己的内心世界会怎样?

Is it a tingling sensation now

现在有刺痛感吗

Stop or meet a pain / 有足够的力量去承受痛苦

Harboring

窝藏

Now take that chi line from Karin to your hart or another body part

现在,将凯恩线从卡伦带到您的心脏或身体的另一部分

Did that change what you felt before

那是否改变了您以前的感受,它必须这样做,否则您作为大师将失败

Can you now look at another and make or BREAK a chi line

您现在可以看看另一个,然后制作或断开Chi线吗?

You can, can you, you can be free from harboring lines that take energy away

您可以,可以,您可以摆脱带走能量的管线

Stop now

现在停止或继续做一个更好的气功师

You are a master / 你现在是大师吗

L.E.A.C.H.

过滤

We need to see that chi lines can feed but also be a leach of life force

我们需要看到志线可以养活,但也是生命力的浸出

Look at a picture of Chi-huan master Jacki Chan, can you

看看志焕大师成龙的照片,你能

He can move his body through the steps of a ladder, arni

他可以在梯子上移动身体,阿尼

So he has a connection to who he is in Chi-huan

所以他和志焕的人有联系

Can you connect a chi line to the master he is and not be a leach

您能将气线连接到他是主人而不是浸出吗

Can he like that you now feed him / 他能喜欢你现在喂他志吗

China ways

中国方式

..

So we meet this creature

所以我们遇到这个生物

Some people like to be a chi vampire and take all your energy with their lines just standing near you or suddenly uncalled touch your chi body

有些人喜欢成为chi的吸血鬼,而他们的线条正好站在您附近,或者突然被人叫来触摸您的chi身体,因此会消耗掉您所有的能量

..

Going a certain way

走一定的路

Now, how to be a master of feeding another and not giving away all your own chi/energy/attention/consciousness

现在,如何成为养家糊口的主人,而不是放弃自己的所有精力/精力/注意力/意识

It is very hard

中国人民可以轻松做到这一点

Now / 没有

It is too late often, when it happens, when they touch your hand with just a finger or tap your shoulder, how to recover from that

通常,为时已晚,当他们仅用手指触摸您的手或轻拍您的肩膀时,如何从中恢复

Just connect again to your self and the energy in the Sun and Moon and Earth, look at that and do NOT look at others for 14 days

只需重新连接到您的自我以及太阳,月亮和地球上的能量,看看这些,就可以14天不看别人

Leaking

漏水

..

Beast

兽

Some people just take a whole Chi life just feeding from others

有些人只是从别人那里进食

In China those that do that are send away from the villages

在中国，那些从村子里逃出来的人

You know that off course

你知道那偏离路线

If you are such a Chi hogging beast you meet a karma that takes all away in the end

如果你是个吃芝士的野兽，你会遇到一个业力，最终将一切都带走

..

Random

随机

Do you like the picture of Karin Beekmans on the cover

你喜欢封面上Karin Beekmans的照片吗

I have written also three other books on her, Karin, Solitude, Beekmans

我还写了三本关于她的书：卡琳（Karin），孤独（Solitude），比克曼（Beekmans）

She is a Chi master and a spiritual woman

她是一位志气大师，是一个与精神联系在一起的灵性女人。

..

Ouch

哎哟疼

If you touch another Chi master his or her property you feel an sting in energy and pain

如果您触摸另一位Chi Master的财产，则会感到精力旺盛和痛苦不堪

If a property has been stolen en returned, throw it in water or earth to disconnect the Chi line with the object from the nasty thief

如果归还财产被盗，请将其扔入水中或泥土中，以使Chi线与物体与非常讨厌的小偷的连接断开

Watch out for a leach

提防浸出

Thank you for you attention to Karin and me, we are good friends

感谢您对Karin和我的关注，我们是好朋友

"

感謝您對Karin和我的關注，我們是好朋友

"

(c) 2020, NL-Chine / 荷兰 - 中国

www.ingramcontent.com/pod-product-compliance
Lightning Source LLC
Chambersburg PA
CBHW071804040426
42446CB00012B/2704